PONDMASTER

A practical guide to creating a

GARDEN POND
AND YEAR-ROUND MAINTENANCE

GRAHAM QUICK

INTERPET PUBLISHING

Author

Graham Quick has been keenly interested in ponds and fish from an early age. Even before leaving school, he spent his spare time working on a commercial fish farm. After leaving school, he created an extremely successful aquatic centre at his family-run garden centre. He is now in the process of setting up an ornamental fish farm.

Published by Interpet Publishing,
Vincent Lane, Dorking, Surrey, RH4 3YX, England.
All rights reserved.
ISBN: 1-902389-96-4

Credits

Created and designed: Ideas into Print,
New Ash Green, Kent DA3 8JD, England.
Production management: Consortium, Poslingford,
Suffolk CO10 8RA, England.
Print production: Sino Publishing House Ltd., Hong Kong.
Printed and bound in China.

Below: Creating a garden pond is a fascinating mix of technology, design, gardening and petcare. Achieving an attractive and viable result brings great satisfaction and can be the start of an obsessive hobby.

Contents

A shallow waterfall makes an ideal birdbath by this peaceful patio pond.

Introduction

A fascination with water

Ever since man started to tend a plot of land, water has played an integral part in gardens. To begin with, ponds were home to edible fish, but the development of coloured fish about 200 years ago was the start of the fishkeeping hobby. The peaceful nature of fish in a well-planted pool provides a welcome relief from the hustle and bustle of daily life. There is nothing more relaxing after a long day at work than sitting by the pond watching the fish swim quietly around, apparently without a care in the world.

Even maintaining a pond can make a welcome change from the daily work routine, although you could argue that this is just the view of a dedicated pondkeeper! However, once you catch the 'bug', you will want to enlarge your first pond and move on to ponds that are even bigger and

better. Many pondkeepers will confess to making three or four ponds before finally settling on their 'perfect' pond. As we all have different ideas of what this means, the possibilities are endless. In this book, we aim to cover all the basic pond-building skills that you will need for your first pond. Three projects are featured here. The first follows the building of a liner pond, from deciding what shape to make it right through to planting up the rockery that houses the filter system. The second project follows the installation of a glass-reinforced plastic shell. The final sequence looks at setting up a quick patio pond in just a few hours.

As you progress to bigger and better ponds, your ideas will become more ambitious, but building techniques change very little – only the quantities increase.

What style of pond?

If you have never kept a pond before, spend a few moments on some important considerations. Having some idea of the style you want will help you to decide on the size and shape of the pond, the type of edging, water features – such as fountains and waterfalls – and even the type of planting.

Remember that there is always maintenance to be done in and around the pond. Try to find time each week to do some work, otherwise the hobby will become a chore and you will lose interest in it.

Below: This water feature and fountain has been created using just wood and a liner. The whole effect is finished with plants to soften the edge and blend a formal-shaped pond into a more informal setting.

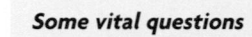

Some vital questions

Is your garden formal in style, with rectangular or square beds and lawn or is it informal in design? Choose a style of pond in keeping with the rest of the garden.

Will small children be playing in the garden?
A raised pond is more difficult for children to fall into accidentally.

How large is the garden?
If it is small, consider installing a patio pond.

What is the pond for?
An ornamental feature with plants and a few fish?
A more specialised pond for koi?
A wildlife pond that will encourage frogs, birds and other creatures into the garden?

Left: A beautifully planted and maintained natural pond that will attract all forms of wildlife to the garden. However, it requires regular maintenance and a fair amount of time to achieve this effect. Such a pond is a welcome addition to any garden.

Left: A planted waterfall can be a real feature. Here, plants break up the edge and help blend the rockwork into the landscape, giving the feeling that it has always been there.

Below: The formal shape and still water create a tranquil environment. This pond requires little maintenance except during the autumn, when the leaves are falling.

Above: This partly raised patio pond adds movement and height to an otherwise low garden. The small edge stops leaves and debris blowing into the water, as well as making a strong contrast to the light-coloured paving.

If you are interested in keeping a mixture of pond fish, such as goldfish, shubunkins, orfe and tench, then the ideal starting size would be a pond measuring about 180x120x60cm deep (72x48x24in) with a capacity of 900 litres (200 gallons). Although smaller ponds do work, they cost about the same to set up yet hold fewer fish. The pond must be at least 60cm (24in) deep to allow the fish to survive a cold winter, but make it deeper if you can.

Right: A typical koi pond has sparse planting and a large open swimming area, with deep water for the fish. Protect the plants from the koi, otherwise the fish will uproot and eat them.

Koi ponds

If you want to keep koi and other large fish, then make the pond as large as possible. Koi, especially, require a great deal of space to thrive. Large ponds are normally easier to look after, and in optimum water conditions, the fish will do well and grow to a good size. It follows that a pond measuring approximately 3x1.8x0.9m (10x6x3 ft) and holding a minimum of 4500 litres (1000 gallons) of water would be a good starting point, but bigger is even better. Bear in mind that a koi pond will need specialised filtration. Consult the relevant books for more information on this subject.

In most garden ponds, fish are the main attraction and any wildlife that turns up is a bonus. But you could create a pond designed to attract wildlife, which means no pumps to suck up the tiny visitors. It is generally felt that fish should not be introduced into a wildlife pond, but this is not natural. Such a pond needs some large animals to rid it of sick or excess populations of pond inhabitants and, most importantly, to eat the mosquitoes. Small native fish are ideal. And the healthier the wildlife population, the more pests they will eat, such as slugs and snails. This in turn means you can use fewer pesticides in your garden. Try to use native plants to enhance the wildlife theme. Most native plants have modern hybrid varieties with better flowers, so look out for these when buying plants for your pond .

Right: Once the plants are established, the fish will have somewhere to hide and feel more secure. Once they have settled down, it does not take long to condition them to feed from your hand.

Below: Plants such as this creeping Jenny (Lysimachia nummularia) *around the edge will encourage frogs to stay nearby during the summer. It also gives them easy access to the pond.*

Siting the pond

The aspect of your garden may influence the type of pond you set up. The ideal position is a semi-shaded one that avoids the midday sun, but receives full sun in the morning and late afternoon. You can create this perfect situation by planting a deciduous tree in the correct place.

If the garden is in full sun, a wildlife pond would do well, as the majority of plants prefer this situation. However, in a sheltered garden, full sun could cause excessive algae growth in summer because the water overheats.

Full shade is not the best position for a pond intended to support plants, as the plants will not receive enough light to flower. However, algal growth will also be slow. The lack of light will also keep the water temperature low in summer. If this is the only site available, it is best suited to a fish-only pond.

Other items to consider when positioning your pond are the availability of water and electricity. Having a water supply plumbed directly to the pond means that you do not need to run the garden hose whenever the pond requires topping up.

Left: *A small weeping tree near the pond provides some afternoon shade. This helps to reduce the amount of light reaching the pond and hence the growth of algae.*

What you need to create a pond

Building a pond is quite an undertaking, and some planning and preparation are essential. When you have decided on the type of pond you are going to build (liner or rigid shell), take some initial measurements. Then make a list of all the materials you will need, research what is available and arrange for any items that you cannot transport to be delivered. Read through the following pages before you start to plan and build to help you decide what to put on the list. Make sure you have all the necessary tools and equipment to make the work as trouble-free as possible.

Above: Choose pond equipment with care. Make sure that pumps and filters are able to cope with the demands put on them. Always read instructions carefully.

Below: The most important objective in building a pond is to make it level. Use a reliable spirit level and straightedge, particularly when installing a rigid shell.

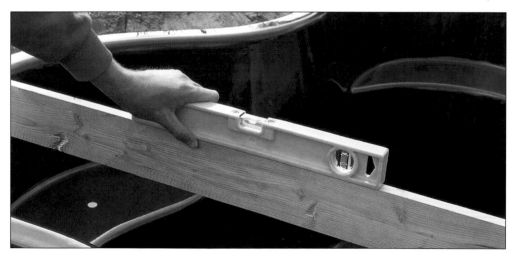

Shopping list

Tools and equipment
Strong digging spade
Spirit level
Straightedge (a length of wood will do)
Wooden pegs
Hammer
Screwdriver
Tape measure
Water meter
Hose
Scissors
Wheelbarrow
Gloves
Trowel for mortar

Materials
Concrete (ready-mix or mix your own)
Pond liner and underlay or rigid shell
Pump and pipework
Hose clips
Filter and UV steriliser
Rockery stone (for waterfall)

Ornament for water return
Paving slabs or other edging material
Cement
Building sand
Gravel
Aquatic soil
Planting baskets

Plants and livestock
Marginal plants
Oxygenators
Floating plants
Water lily
Pond fish
Plants for the rockery

Extras for all ponds
Test kits
Fish food
Plant food
Net to catch fish and remove leaves
Net to cover pond in autumn

Mimulus lewisii, a beautiful marginal plant for summer colour.

Your early decisions regarding the shape, size and depth of your pond will have a crucial bearing on its final appearance and how easy it is to maintain, so it is vital to make the right choices.

Shape
When deciding on a shape for the pond, make sure that it fits in with the rest of the garden. In a natural garden, a square pond with a brick surround might look out of place, whereas an oval pond with a natural stone surround would blend in well. A simple shape such as a square will be easy to excavate and line. Once finished, you can subtly alter its appearance by your choice of edging. A larger overhang creates a different effect to a small one. This technique can also work very effectively with more complex shapes. If possible, draw a simple scale plan of the garden and mark in the pond shape. This will also help you to decide its eventual size.

Size
The size of the pond is mainly determined by the surrounding site, be it a small patio or a large garden. Generally speaking, the rule is the bigger, the better. Another factor to consider is the type of fish you intend to keep; larger fish will require large ponds.

Depth
The depth of the pond is another important consideration. If it is too shallow – less than 45cm (18in) – the temperature of the water will vary from day to day. Neither fish nor plants can tolerate this state of affairs very well and it also encourages algae growth. The minimum depth should be at least 60cm (24in) and ideally 75cm (30in) to ensure that the fish and plants can survive the winter. In a cold climate, make the pond even deeper. For koi and larger fish, a pond needs to be 120cm (48in) deep or more for them to stay in all season.

Check the site
Before starting to dig any holes, you must make sure that there are no services, such as gas, electricity or water, or any drains running across the area to be excavated. If in doubt, check with your service providers.

Above: To mark out a circular pond, hammer a round post into the centre of the site and place a loop of string over it. To achieve a pond of a certain size, make the loop equal to half the desired diameter (the radius) of the pond. Loop the other end of the string to the neck of a plastic bottle filled with dry sand. Keeping the string taut, invert the bottle so that the sand flows out smoothly. Walk around the post leaving a sand mark as you go.

Left: Use the same principle to mark out an oval shape. However, instead of one post in the centre of the site, use two posts, accurately spaced. Loop the string around both posts, keep it taut and mark out the shape with sand.

Marking out an informal shape

Use a garden hose to outline your design, making sure that the shape is not too complex, otherwise, it will be difficult to line and edge. Once outlined, look at the shape from all angles and from an upstairs window if possible. This will give you an idea of how the finished pond will look and how well the shape blends in with the overall design of your garden.

This would not be an easy shape to line as you would have difficulty folding the liner around the edge where the two circles join.

Although this figure of eight is a popular shape, it may not look very neat when finished because of the many pleats needed to fold the liner into place.

A crescent shape is easy to line and fits into most gardens, particularly in corner sites.

Choose a level site with good drainage. This will help to prevent ground water lifting the liner in wet weather.

Use a brightly coloured hose or rope to mark out the line, as this will give you a better idea of the shape.

Although it is not essential, laying a concrete collar around the edge of the pond at this stage will make the remainder of the installation process much easier. Firstly, it will provide an even surface to work from, and later in the construction process it makes a level platform on which to place your chosen edging material. Finally, and most importantly, it will ensure that the edging is safely anchored when people stand on it.

How the collar works

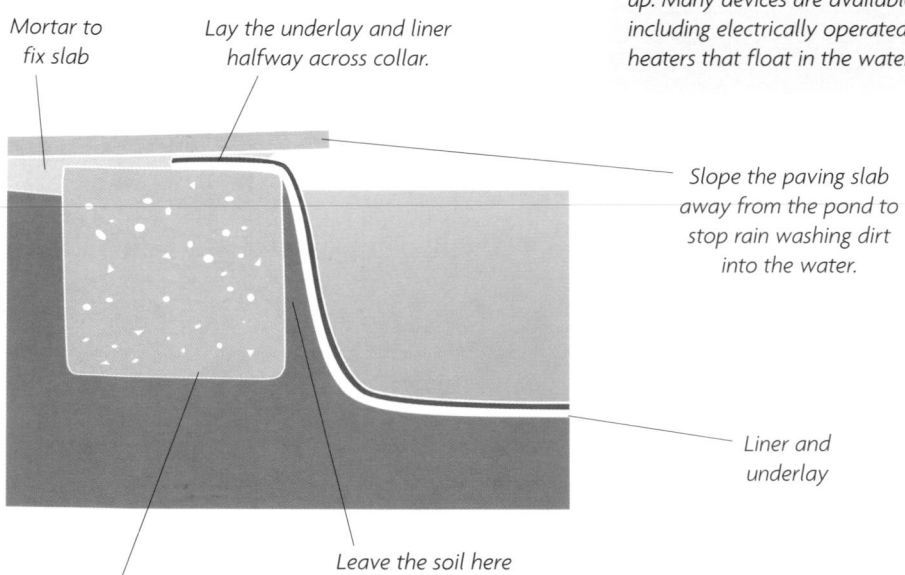

Mortar to fix slab

Lay the underlay and liner halfway across collar.

Slope the paving slab away from the pond to stop rain washing dirt into the water.

Liner and underlay

Concrete collar

Leave the soil here as added protection for the liner.

Protecting the collar in winter

Since the collar forms a rigid boundary around the pond at and below water level, it will prevent ice from expanding outwards as it freezes. To avoid ice breaking the collar, use some form of anti-icing device in the water during the winter to relieve the pressure that builds up. Many devices are available, including electrically operated heaters that float in the water.

Levelling the collar

1 Level the tops of the posts with a straightedge and spirit level. Do this all around the trench.

Wooden posts, each 50x50mm (2x2in)

2 Lay concrete to the top of the posts and level it. Even if the ground slopes, the collar will be level.

Leave the posts in the concrete.

Digging out the collar

1 To make the collar, excavate a shallow trench, working round the outside of the pond shape. Make the trench 13-15cm (5-6in) deep. Work evenly around the shape once, making the trench as wide as the spade.

Use a strong spade with a sharp edge.

Leave the hosepipe in place until you have dug all round it once.

At this point you will need to decide whether you are going to build a rockery, as this will determine where you place the spoil. When building a rockery or waterfall, place the turf on the bottom and keep some topsoil separate to finish off the rockery and provide good soil for the plants.

Hints and tips

Try to choose a period of settled weather for the work. If necessary, cover the area with a water-proof sheet. Bear in mind that in winter making a pond may be interrupted by rain. In summer, the ground can be hard and more difficult to dig.

2 Measure the width of the trench and use the spade as a guide to mark out the width. It is easier to remove excess soil later than replace it.

3 Dig round the trench once more. The aim is to make the trench 5cm (2in) narrower than the edging slabs so that they overhang the water by this amount. This will hide the liner and shield it from sunlight, thus reducing ultraviolet light damage.

When you have dug out the trench for the collar, the next stage is to fill it with concrete. You can buy ready-mixed concrete in small bags, which is ideal if you are only making a small collar or you do not want to mix your own. All you need to do is pour the contents out and use them as shown here. (Although all the ingredients should be mixed evenly, it may be a good idea to stir the dry mix before use.) Alternatively, make up a concrete mix consisting of four parts of all-in aggregate (sharp sand and stones up to 20mm/0.75in in size, also known as ballast) to one part of cement powder. Mix well until the result is an even colour throughout.

Above: *Pour out piles of all-in aggregate and cement in a ratio of four to one. Use a piece of plywood or plastic.*

Below: *Turn the aggregate and cement powder into each other until you achieve an even colour.*

Safety first

Concrete mix and other building materials are heavy. Take care when lifting heavy bags that you do not strain your back. As with all cement-based products, avoid breathing in the dust or exposing your skin to them. Always follow the manufacturer's directions and wear a protective mask or clothes as recommended.

How much concrete mix do I need to buy ?

Once you have finished digging out the trench, you can work out how much concrete mix you need by taking the following measurements and doing a few simple calculations.

1 Measure the total length of the trench in metres, ie around the pond. A good way of doing this is to trail string in the trench until you arrive at your starting point and then measure the length of string you have used.
2 Measure the width of the trench in metres.
3 Measure the depth of the trench in metres, but remember to take off the depth of the edging slabs.
4 Multiply all these figures together to arrive at the amount of mix needed in cubic metres.

Example:
Length of trench around pond: 15 metres
Width of trench: 0.45 metres
Depth of trench: 0.2 metres
Take away the depth of the slabs
  (0.15 metres)
0.2-0.05=0.15 metres

Multiply all three figures together:
15x0.45x0.15=1.01
So you need just over one cubic metre of concrete mix to fill the trench.

Adding the concrete

1 *Lay the dry concrete mix in the trench, levelling the surface as you work your way round. The aim is to make the surface of the collar at a depth such that when you add your edging slabs, the top surface is about 2cm (0.8in) below the level of the surrounding lawn. This will enable you to mow over the edge without damaging it or the mower.*

Note: *The levelling method shown on page 16 is not shown in this sequence of photographs.*

page 16

▶ *Hints and tips*

Using a dry concrete mix to fill the trench means that you can take as long as you need to mix and use all the concrete required, thus avoiding the risk of weak joints between each batch.

Do not excavate the centre section yet as it is acting as an inner wall to the trench and supporting the concrete mix while it dries.

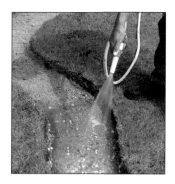

2 *Water the concrete mix well. You may need to agitate the surface to encourage the water to penetrate to the base. Level off as you go, but leave a rough finish. Allow the concrete to dry overnight. In hot weather, cover the collar with a wet sheet to slow the drying process and prevent cracking.*

Do not pack the dry concrete down hard as this will stop water reaching the lower part of the mix.

Once the concrete collar has dried out, you can start to dig out the central cavity of the pond. When digging close to the collar, do not use it as a lever to remove soil as it will break the edge of the concrete. Excavate it to the required depth (see page 14), remembering to leave shelves 20cm (8in) deep and wide to support baskets of pond plants. To stop the sides collapsing, slope the sides of the pond into the centre by about 10cm (4in) for every 30cm (12in) of depth. In loose soils, you may need to apply a gentler gradient. There is no need to create three or four different depths in the pool. This makes lining it very awkward and increases the number of pleats and creases that will be visible in the finished result.

Safety first

When digging, wear strong boots and use the correct tools. Take it at a sensible pace – it is easier to dig out a smaller amount each time than fewer large ones. Take regular breaks, and in hot weather drink plenty of fluids.

Side view of marginal shelf

The basket should rest securely on the shelf, just below the water level.

Make the shelf 2cm (0.8in) deeper than the deepest basket.

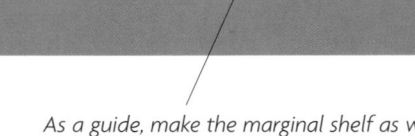

As a guide, make the marginal shelf as wide as a large planting basket plus 10cm (4in).

1 Start digging at one end and remove the turf and roots to a depth of about 10cm (4in) to expose the topsoil. Avoid standing directly on the collar if you can. You can protect it with boards and this also provides a path for the wheelbarrow.

2 Mark out where the shelves are to go. Leave them larger and not as deep as necessary, in case the edge falls away while you are digging the rest of the pond. It is much easier to dig away more soil than to rebuild it. Remove the topsoil and keep it separate for later use. Dig out the rest of the pond to the required depth and shape, remembering to slope the sides as you work. Make the base as flat as possible to ensure a good fit when you add the liner.

3 Excavate roughly to the required shape and depth. Take a moment to stand back and check that you have put the shelves in the correct place. Do not make any shelves under the waterfall. Make the base as level as possible.

Use turf as a base for the rockery, cover it with subsoil and a final layer of topsoil. Remember to compact the soil as you go, otherwise the rockery will sink as the soil settles.

4 Now you can start the final shaping of the shelves. They should be 2-4cm (0.8-1.6in) deeper than the baskets you are going to use. The shelf should be level or slope towards the outer edge of the pond to stop baskets falling into the pond.

The base of the pond should be as level as possible as this will affect the fit of the liner.

It is important to use a good underlay to protect your liner, because once the edging is complete, it will be the most difficult item to change if it is punctured. Although sand is often recommended as an underlay, it will not stop roots or stones making their way to the liner, and if water gets behind the liner, the sand is washed away. Thin builder's polythene is also sold as underlay, but it is not suitable because water can become trapped between the liner and the polythene. And roots will have no difficulty penetrating polythene.

Below: Spun underlays are by far the best, as they allow water to move through them. This prevents water from being trapped between the liner and underlay and stops roots penetrating the liner. Buy more than you need so that you have some to spare for the waterfall.

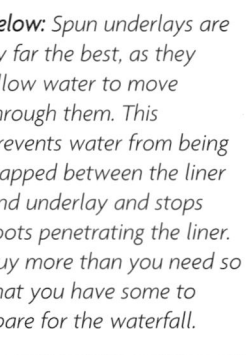

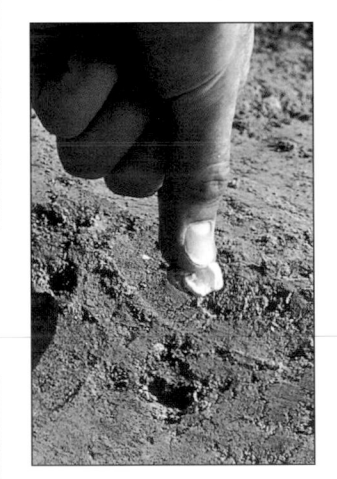

Below: Remove all stones and any roots from nearby trees. If you stood on a stone such as this while installing your liner, you could puncture the liner before you have even added water to the pond.

Above: Before installing the underlay, sweep the collar to remove any stones that could fall into the pond.

WATER PRESSURE

Left: Even a small pond of 1000 litres (220 gallons) holds 1000kg (2200lbs) of water, so it is important to remove any items that could puncture the lining.

Water leaks through split in plastic

Installing the underlay

This underlay material is lightweight and easy for one person to position in the excavation.

1 Depending on the size of the pond, you will need to use more than one width of underlay material. The overlap should be about 15cm (6in) to stop roots finding their way through. Pull the first sheet of underlay over the pond and position other sheets until there are no bare patches of soil between them.

2 Carefully push the underlay into all the curves and corners. This ensures a good fit.

3 Once in place, roughly trim the underlay so that it overlaps the collar by half its width.

4 Soak the underlay to hold it in position while you put the liner in place. Soaking only works with material underlays.

The liner is the most important part of the pond, and so there is no point in buying a cheap one. It is the most difficult part to replace if a fault occurs. The best colour is black. Although it may not look right when you are installing it, black has many advantages. The most important of these is its lifespan in sunlight, as it is least affected by ultraviolet light.

Measuring your pond for underlay and liner

Measuring your pond for the liner could not be simpler. Using a flexible tape measure, start about 30cm (12in) from the edge of the collar at one end of the pond and follow the contours down to the base, across the bottom and up the other side. Repeat this for the width. Remember to measure at the longest and widest parts of the pond. By this method you will arrive at a very accurate measurement of the length and width of the pond and can avoid wasting excess liner.

Right: When you get your pond liner home, check it carefully for tears and imperfections; once you have installed it, you will not be able to remove it easily. Replace the liner in its packaging and store it in a safe place until you are ready to use it.

This allowance gives you a margin for trimming the liner to size.

Types of pond liner

Many grades of pond liners are available. The three most popular are butyl (isobutylene isoprene rubber), EPDM (ethylene propylene diene rubber membrane) and PVC (polyvinyl chloride). The newer mixes of PVC are now as flexible as butyl, as well as being stronger and lighter. You can buy them in very large sizes from most water garden centres. For large liners, butyl has the advantage that it can be welded on site quite easily. Two-colour pond lining materials with a reinforcing layer are not as flexible as the above products.

Butyl pond liner

PVC liner

Installing the liner

1 Unroll the liner next to the pond and make sure it is the right way round. With a person at each end, drag the liner over the hole and slowly lower it in. Leave an even overlap all round the edge.

With large liners you will need at least one other person to help you with the installation. The more people, the easier it is.

When placing the liner on the underlay, make sure the underlay has not fallen into the pond, otherwise the liner will have no protection.

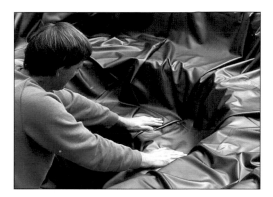

2 Once the liner is in place, you can get into the pond (remember to remove your shoes) and help the liner to mould to the more intricate shapes. This will also give you an idea of where the pleats and folds will be in the finished pond.

You may see suggestions that you should place rocks around the edge of the liner and let it stretch into place as you add water to the pond. This rarely works in practice. More often, one side slides in before the other, taking the underlay in with it and then depositing the water into the unprotected hole, creating a great mess. To make life easier, lower the liner into the excavation and push it into the shape as best you can. When you have an even overlap around the edge, add water to fill the pond.

1 Once the liner is in place, use a hose to fill the pond to a depth of about 15cm (6in). As the pond fills, adjust the liner carefully to remove as many creases as possible. This will determine how the rest of the liner fits in. Remember that the bottom of the pond is the most visible part, so try to make the liner in this area as smooth as you can.

Using a water meter

As you fill the pond for the first time, it is a good idea to use a water meter to measure the capacity of your pond. Simply fit this device onto your hosepipe and it will record the water flow through it. Knowing how much water your pond holds will be of great use later on. Firstly, it will help you to choose appropriate pumps and filtration systems for your pond's capacity. Secondly, it helps you to estimate with confidence the quantities of additives and treatments that you may need to correct an imbalance in water chemistry or treat the fishes in the pond.

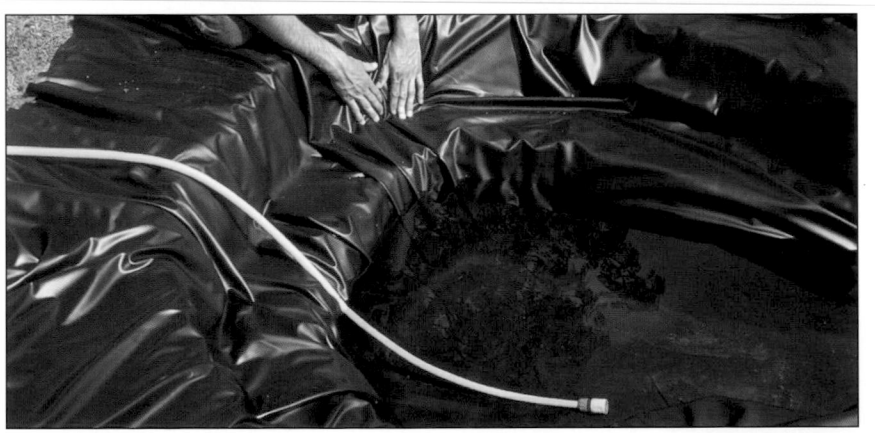

2 As the water level rises, pull the liner into position to reduce the pleats and folds to a minimum. This will take some time and is quite hard work, but it is well worth doing the best you can. Fill the pond slowly at this stage so that you have plenty of time to adjust the liner.

Trimming the pond liner

With the liner installed and the pond reasonably full of water, trim off the excess liner so that the remaining liner covers half the collar. If in doubt, cut too little off the first time around and more later if you need to. Remember you cannot add it back if you cut too much off.

This is the end of the process of excavating and lining the pond. Now that the pond has water in it, it is vital to cover it, so that there is no danger of people or animals falling into it while it is unattended, particularly at night.

You can use large offcuts of liner for the waterfall (see page 33).

Hints and tips

Once you have cut around the liner, place some slabs around the edges to stop it sliding or blowing into the pond.

LINER POND – Edging the pond

Edging the pond can be one of the most time-consuming parts of the project. But it is time well spent, because it not only secures the liner, but also conceals it from view. Try to choose an edging material that will blend in with the garden and is within your budget. Brimming pools look the best, so the finished edge should be as close as possible to the water surface. This has two beneficial effects: it hides any pleats in the liner near the surface and protects the liner from sunlight, which degrades it over time. Another point to think about is how much foot traffic is going to use the edge. A man-made surface, such as concrete paving, normally lasts better than natural stone. If the traffic is heavy, a wider area of paving will reduce the effect on surrounding lawns.

1 When mixing mortar for the edging, use a strong mix; the last thing you want is loose paving around the pond. The mortar should consist of 1 part cement to 4 parts of building sand.

2 Mix the sand and cement thoroughly until it is an even colour throughout. Do this on a clean plastic or wooden board to avoid unwanted debris being mixed into the mortar. Remove any stones or lumps in the mix.

3 Once the dry ingredients are thoroughly mixed, start to add water a little at a time. (You can also mix in a plasticiser at this stage to make the mortar easier to work with.) At first, it is best to make the mix too dry rather than too sloppy; you can easily add more water, but it is difficult to dry out wet mortar.

4 Check the mix for consistency and keep adding water and mixing until you have achieved a smooth texture. Pick up some mortar on the trowel to test it out – it should stay on the blade and not be loose or too powdery.

5 Lay the slabs around the pond without fixing them down to check that they fit and overhang the pond sufficiently to cover the liner edge. Before laying any mortar, pull the liner taut to avoid any unnecessary pleats. Lay a good bed of mortar on the liner and collar.

6 Leave a few of the loose slabs in place to keep the liner securely in position as you work. Use the trowel to spread out the mortar and aim to cover an area larger than the slab to be laid. The mortar bed should be a consistent depth – about 2.5cm (1in) is fine for these slabs.

Other edging materials

You can edge the pond with brick pavers but, being smaller, these need a more secure fixing method than slabs. Cobbles set in a cement bed are very attractive but are unsuitable for walking on; use them intermingled with slabs for walking areas. Wood is very easy to fix around the edge, but make sure that the sealant and preservative used are fish-safe.

7 Lower the slab carefully onto the bed of mortar. Be careful not to trap your fingers between the slabs as you do this. Try not to push the slab into place, as this will spread the mortar over a larger area and make the bed thinner.

8 Place a straightedge and spirit level across the slab and check the level as you tamp down with the handle of a club hammer or rubber mallet. Do not use a metal surface, as it will damage the finish.

9 Tape a small section of wood under one end of the spirit level to create a fall of about 1cm per 30cm (0.4in per 12in) away from the pond. This will stop rain washing dirt across the slabs and into the water.

LINER POND – Finishing the edging

1 When laying consecutive slabs, try to leave an even gap between them, as you will need to point the gap later on. As you lay the slabs, you can change the shape of the pond edging by varying the overhang of each slab.

Right: In our main sequence we have chosen to lay the slabs square on, but if you follow the curve of the pond you will need to cut infill pieces, as here. An electric stone cutter makes this easier.

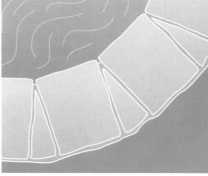

Cutting slabs

When cutting slabs to fit into corners, work on a soft, even surface, such as a bed of sand, to spread the force exerted by the hammer without shattering the slab. Gently score a cutting line across the slab and then hammer down with more force across the centre. The slab should break cleanly along the scored line.

Right: As you complete the pond edging, you will need to install a short length of plastic pipe across the collar and between two slabs to provide a safe exit for the electrical cable connected to the pond pump. If you intend to have lights in or around the pond, you will need an extra cable exit point.

2 Using the paving that has been cut to size, lay a deep bed of mortar and twist the paving into place. As before, tamp the slab into place with the hammer handle and check for level – it should follow the fall of the other slabs away from the pond.

As you lay the slabs, keep checking that they are level in relation to each other and to the water. If the land rises at one end of the site, as here, you will find that the final paving slab is below the level of the adjacent ground. You can make any adjustments to the landscaping afterwards.

3 When the mortar has cured for a day, start to point between the slabs to finish the paving. Use a 4 to 1 mix of sand to cement for strength.

4 As the mortar starts to dry, use a short length of hose to force mortar into the gaps between the slabs. This will compress the mortar and leave a smooth finish to each joint.

Deciding how big to make the waterfall and controlling how fast the water will run down it can be difficult and can cause many problems. Too fast a flow, and the pond will look like a spa bath; too slow, and the filter will not work correctly. The factors to take into consideration include the volume of the pond, the width of the flow of water over the waterfall and the maximum recommended flow rate for the biological filter and UV unit. You can calculate the volume of the pond using a water meter (see page 26). The recommended flow rate for filters is at least half the volume of the pond per hour. A water flow 15cm (6in) wide and 0.5cm (0.2in) deep will cycle 1300 to 1500 litres (285-330 gallons) per hour. Consult the manufacturer's guidance for recommended flow rates for the filter and UV unit.

1 Install the filter system before you build the waterfall so that you can fit the outlet from the filter into the waterfall. Dig out a hole larger than required for the biological filter and clear an area next to it to take the ultraviolet (UV) light unit. Run a conduit to the UV unit for the electric cable.

2 Place a paving slab smooth side uppermost into the cavity prepared for the biological filter and check it for level both ways. This slab will provide a flat level surface for the biofilter to sit on.

3 Place the biofilter box onto the slab and check for level.

4 Fit the lid onto the filter box to stop soil falling in as you work around it. Backfill around the filter with soil, taking care not to compact it too hard, otherwise it could press on the sides of the box and deform the shape.

5 Position a half-slab in the area you have cleared for the UV unit. Stand the unit on the slab, making sure it is level.

6 Now that the filter is installed, you can excavate the waterfall profile. Remember to dig deeper than required to allow for the rockwork and mortar. As you work near the edge of the pond, avoid stepping on the new paving to allow it to cure fully.

The slabs overhang the water sufficiently to disguise the liner and protect the edges of it from the damaging effects of the sun.

7 Cover all the exposed soil of the excavation with offcuts of underlay, using two thicknesses over the collar to protect the liner. Soak the underlay into place before laying the liner on top.

8 Lay a generous piece of pond liner onto the underlay, allowing plenty of overlap to pull up behind the rocks when you position them.

Choose your rockery stones in a colour that complements that of the paving slabs and any other stone used in the garden. Remember that water will be running over the stones and they need to be hard enough not to wear away. This may sound obvious, but there are some very soft stones on the market, such as tufa (a very soft limestone), which dissolves over very short periods of time. As they dissolve, they increase the pH of the water beyond levels tolerated by fish. If you are not sure whether a rock is suitable, put a piece in a container and pour a little vinegar (an acid) onto it. If it fizzes quickly, it is alkaline and not ideal for a pond. If it produces small bubbles, it is hard enough not to affect pH levels. (See page 48 for more on pH.)

Placing rocks in the path of the water creates a natural meandering effect and slows down the water flow.

Below: *This top view shows the water flowing from the biofilter down the waterfall and into the pond.*

Biofilter

1 With some of the outer rocks in place, pass the filter feed hose beneath the liner and underlay. If there are any sharp rock edges touching the hose, wedge in extra layers of underlay to prevent damage to the hose.

2 Now lay down the rocks that will form the last fall into the pond. They need to be relatively flat to ensure an even and relatively slow-moving flow of water across them. This lessens the rippling effect and makes seeing into the water much easier.

Take care when lifting heavy stones that you do not strain your back or drop them and injure yourself.

Remember to align the strata (visible lines running through the rocks) across the waterfall to reflect how they would appear in a natural setting.

How much water does the waterfall use?

This pond holds 2300 litres (505 gallons). The maximum width of the waterfall is 20cm (8in) and the filter can handle 2500 litres (550 gallons) per hour. To calculate the amount of water required for the waterfall, divide the actual width of the waterfall (20cm) by 15 (average width) then multiply by 1400 (average water cycle – see page 32).

Thus, 20÷15x1400=1886 litres (415 gallons) per hour. This is within the capabilities of the filter and the pond. Using a filter larger than required means you can achieve the desired water flow with less maintenance.
A smaller filter would suit the pond, but its flow rate of 1250 litres (275 gallons) per hour would not cope with the waterfall.

Avoid a straight water flow from top to bottom. It is better to start by pushing the water one way, then encouraging it slowly back to the centre line and finally across to the other side.

It is always difficult to work out how much stone you will need, but you could try laying out a mock-up at the stone merchant's and then adding a few extra pieces to extend the rockery into the garden. When your rock has been delivered, wash it well to remove any dust or soil. These not only make the pond dirty, but also stop the mortar adhering to the stone. If the thought of handling heavy rock is too daunting, you can also buy 'fake' rocks made of concrete and fibre glass that are much lighter and easier to use. Their only disadvantage is the lack of a variety in the shapes. Complete waterfall sections are also available as plastic mouldings (see page 54).

Arranging the rockery stones may take more than one attempt. Before you even think of cementing them into place, lay them roughly in position, stand back and examine the result from all angles. Move any stones you are not happy with and consult other members of the family for advice; what looks good to you may not look right to other people. Once you are happy with the effect and the water flow pattern, prepare to bed them down permanently.

2 As the rocks are bedded down, fill in the gaps with mortar. If you are using a different colour stone, you can buy additives to add to the mortar to match your stonework.

1 Remove one rock at a time, lay a bed of mortar in its place and then push the rock into it to bed it down. Do not twist the rock from side to side as this could puncture the liner.

3 As you fill gaps between rocks, large areas of mortar may become obvious. Fill these spaces with pieces of rock, which will not only hide the mortar, but also break up the water flow.

4 Using a small pointing trowel, push mortar into all the gaps. The aim is to prevent water flowing behind the rocks and to ensure that they are all firmly fixed in place.

5 As you work your way up to the filter, make the fall away from the outlet as steep as possible. This avoids the risk of a blockage, which could cause the overflow to empty the pond. As with all gravity-exit filters, the water must flow out of the box and down the hill. If you have enough space, you can build a taller rockery to hide the filter; otherwise, hide it with a group of plants.

Electrical connection

As with all electrics in the garden, you should protect the cables from contact with abrasive or sharp surfaces. The plastic pipe under the paving should lead to a correctly installed power supply and switch that incorporates a circuit breaker. If in doubt, ask a qualified electrician to install the connection.

Below: When fitting the pump, feed the power cable through the plastic pipe you fixed under the paving.

6 When connecting the hose to the biofilter and UV unit, fit the largest bore hose the pump will accept. Use a flexible hose for tighter turns and secure all the connections with stainless steel clips.

7 When installing the pump in the pond, turn off the electricity supply while your hands are in the water. It is a good idea to wrap some waterproof tape over the hose clip in case it catches the liner and tears it.

The pump, ultraviolet light (UV) steriliser and filter

When selecting your pond pump, consider the following factors: is the pump repairable? Are spares easy to obtain? Although these may seem trivial considerations, there is nothing more annoying than not being able to repair a pump that is just out of warranty. The other important factor is the electrical consumption of the pump. Better build-quality generally means lower running costs but a higher purchase price. The difference in running costs can be considerable, so check before you buy. Also examine the warranty, as some exclude moving parts. As this is the most important part of a pump, such a warranty is worthless.

Above: When installing a pump, always use the largest pipe recommended and fit it directly to the pump; extra fittings will slow down the flow of water.

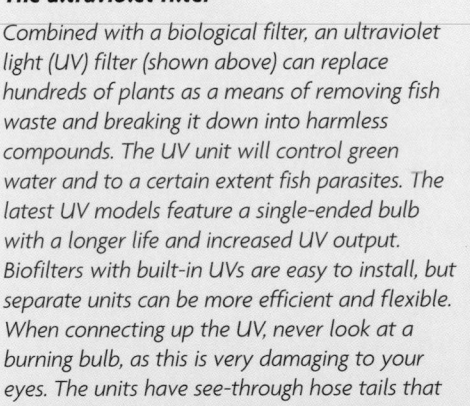

The filter strainer should exclude any particles that could block the pump impeller.

If you do not use the fountain, you can remove the filter foams.

The pump should be easy to disassemble for maintenance and cleaning.

The ultraviolet filter

Combined with a biological filter, an ultraviolet light (UV) filter (shown above) can replace hundreds of plants as a means of removing fish waste and breaking it down into harmless compounds. The UV unit will control green water and to a certain extent fish parasites. The latest UV models feature a single-ended bulb with a longer life and increased UV output. Biofilters with built-in UVs are easy to install, but separate units can be more efficient and flexible. When connecting up the UV, never look at a burning bulb, as this is very damaging to your eyes. The units have see-through hose tails that glow when the bulb is working (shown right).

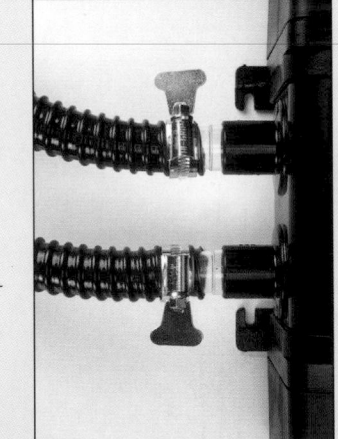

Anatomy of a filter

The basic filter works in three stages. In the first stage – coarse mechanical filtration – the larger particles, such as fragments of leaves that have passed through the pump, are removed in the plastic media. As the water spreads out and slows down, the particles drop to the floor of the filter. During the second stage – fine filtration – layers of foam remove small and then fine suspended particles. In the third and final stage – the main biological stage – bacteria convert the fish waste into harmless plant food. The gravel and plastic pieces provide a large surface area with a good flow rate of water and plenty of oxygen for many millions of beneficial bacteria to thrive. Finally, clean water returns to the pond.

This pipe directs water to the base of the filter, from where it flows up and out of the exit pipe.

Different grades of foam trap floating particles in the water.

Exit pipe to waterfall

A small length of return pipe is supplied and can be used to extend the exit pipe.

Plastic media replaces the gravel in older filters. It offers a large surface area for bacteria to colonise and allows good water flow.

The gravel trays hold down the foam layers and act as a second stage biofilter.

What does a pond filter do?

Quite simply, a pond filter is a cesspit for fish waste. As you feed the fish they produce fecal matter, which would break down in a natural pond, where nature has limited the stocking level. However, in a garden pond the waste level rises, producing unsuitable conditions in which the fish would eventually die. The pond filter breaks down these products into nitrates, which at low levels are harmless compounds that plants can readily use as plant food for growing. A filter does not replace plants, but used correctly it can maintain clean water conditions for the fishes.

Above: *Wash the gravel thoroughly and place the gravel trays on top of the foam layers to hold them in place so that the maximum amount of water flows through the foam and not around the edge.*

When adding the main filter and UV steriliser to the rockery, remember to install a conduit to the UV's position so you can safely run electricity to it. Secure all water pipes with stainless steel hose clips to stop any pipes becoming loose. It make no sense to risk the pond emptying and the pump burning out for the cost of good-quality hose clips. Place the UV unit on a level base that will not flood with water when it rains and that allows easy access for regular maintenance, such as replacing the bulb and cleaning the quartz bulb cover. In regions with cold winters you must drain the UV unit and store it where it is protected from frost – left in place and full of water, it will split as the water inside it freezes.

How the water flows

Right: When you have installed the pipework to the main filter and UV unit, you can turn on the pump and start the water flowing over the waterfall. As it runs, you can see if you need to reduce the flow or not. In most cases, a turnover rate of the half the pond volume per hour is normally acceptable for the filters, but you may require more flow down the waterfall. If so, remember not to exceed the filter's maximum recommended flow rate.

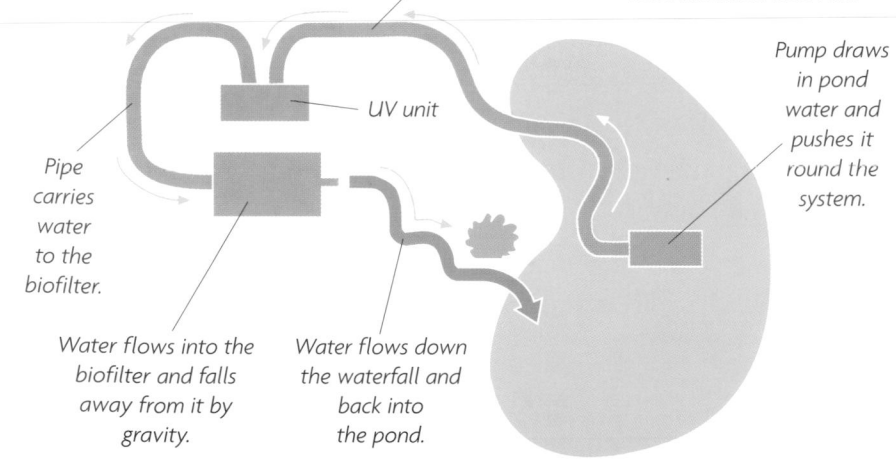

Pipe carries water to the UV unit.

UV unit

Pipe carries water to the biofilter.

Pump draws in pond water and pushes it round the system.

Water flows into the biofilter and falls away from it by gravity.

Water flows down the waterfall and back into the pond.

Trimming the waterfall liner

With the pump running, check the waterfall for any obvious leaks and trim off any excess liner that is visible along the edges. You may need to add more mortar in areas where it is not high enough to contain the water flow. If you need to do this, turn off the pump and use quick-setting cement (follow the instructions on the packet). Wait until the cement is dry before turning the pump on again. If the flow runs to one side, place rocks in the flowing water to divert it across the waterfall to achieve an even and satisfactory effect. If the flow is still not quite right when you have completely finished the waterfall, do not panic! You can add extra rocks in the path of the water and secure them with aquarium sealant.

Hints and tips

Before trimming off any liner, run the waterfall for a few hours. This will show up any leaks as the surrounding soil becomes darker with the dampness. When running the waterfall for the first time, keep a careful check on the water level in the pond. If there is a major leak, the pond pump may run out of water and be damaged.

1 Trim the liner with scissors and only cut off small pieces at a time. You can easily trim more off but it is very difficult to join pieces back on. Work from the top to the bottom and check the effect of your trimming on the water flow.

2 Follow the edge of the waterfall as you trim, making sure you leave enough liner behind to contain the water inside and to hold back the soil on the other side. The aim is to stop soil washing down and turning the pond murky.

3 Using the topsoil you put aside during the pond excavation, cover the rockery and fill up the pockets between the stones right up to the edge of the waterfall. This is where you will be adding a range of garden plants to hide any liner that is still showing and to soften the sharp edges of the rocks.

As you will soon find out, water plants will prosper with little if any care. With a few exceptions, nearly all water plants are hardy perennials and most have a vigorous growth habit. Raising new plants by cuttings or division is very easy to do and is a good way of slowing down the growth of the parent plants. You can use rigid perforated plastic baskets for water plants or the type made of a flexible synthetic material. Flexible containers are easy to mould into odd corners of the pond to produce tighter clumps of plants and they restrict the fast-growing plant roots. Other plus points are that they will sit on uneven surfaces without rocking and the soft material cannot damage the liner as rigid ones can.

Planting your baskets

When planting your pond baskets, put vigorous ones on their own and pot up less vigorous plants together. Use a good aquatic soil or soil from a neglected part of the garden (not alkaline). Do not add any general garden fertilisers, as they are water soluble and will dissolve in the pond and encourage blanketweed and green water. You can buy a special fertiliser that goes into the basket and lasts for the whole season. Once planted, cover the soil with 2.5cm (1in) of gravel to stop fish disturbing the plants.

Above: *Water each basket before placing it in the pond to wash off any excess soil that would otherwise cloud the water. Lower the basket – here one of the flexible types – slowly into the water onto the shelf. If the shelf is too deep, raise the basket on a small slab or brick.*

Left: *When planting the pond, try to emulate nature by placing tall plants around the outer margins – not just across the back. As well as offering shade, these tall plants will hinder predators fishing along the clear edge.*

Adding water lilies

Planting a water lily is easier than choosing the colour and size you want. Before choosing a water lily, be sure to take into account the size of the pond, the water depth and the amount of sun it receives. When buying a lily, look for rich green leaves (not brown slimy ones) with no yellowing at the edges. The crown should be hard, as this is where the plant stores its food during winter. The roots should be growing through the sides of the basket; newly potted ones are not the best buys because they can take some time to settle down again. Good aquatic centres will display the plants in shallow tanks at least 30cm (12in) deep. Avoid water lilies kept in plastic boxes but not in water. These can dry out and may even get mould on them, from which they rarely recover. If a particular plant looks healthy, then it probably is; if it looks poorly, do not buy it.

Larger plants for an instant display

Many aquatic centres sell larger, more mature specimens of water lilies – often with flowers – in 10 litre pots or larger. If you cannot wait a year or two for smaller ones to mature, these larger plants are a good buy that offer instant surface coverage and the bonus of flowers, too. The range of varieties available in larger sizes tends to be limited, so do not buy one if it is not the variety or size you really want. Planting an unsuitable one may cause problems and disappointment later on if it grows too large or does not fit into the colour scheme of the pond. If you are in any doubt, be patient and wait for a smaller one to mature.

1 When you first put the water lily in its basket on the bottom of your pond, the leaves may not be able to float on the surface. You can use a clean, upturned plastic pot to raise the lily up to the correct height. A black pot will be less visible in the water.

2 To wash surplus soil from the basket, make sure that the lily is thoroughly watered before you place it in the pond. Also add a generous layer of gravel to the surface to stop your fish digging the soil out and disturbing the plant as it becomes established.

3 With the lily in the pond, the leaves should be about 4cm (1.5in) below the water to allow them to grow to the surface. Depending on the temperature and variety, you will need to lower the lily every month so that eventually the basket is on the bottom.

Buying plants for the pond is not always as easy as it should be. Many aquatic centres only stock the plants that are in flower at the time; choosing just these would provide a flowering display that would be all over in a month. Make a list of plants that you would like and try to choose ones that spread their flowering time out over the season. That way you will always have some flowering interest to keep up your pond display. A good mix of colours is available, although a large number of aquatic plant flowers are yellow. Look out for plants with different leaf shapes and colours to add more interest around the pond. Using low-growing water plants will soften the paving edge and create hiding places for young fish.

▶ *Hints and tips*

When planting oxygenators, always remove the lead strip that is wrapped around the stems, as this can cause the plants to rot off just above the strip. Also, it is best to avoid any heavy metals in the pond, as they poise a possible health hazard to the fish.

Right: Plant oxygenators, such as these Elodea canadensis, *in baskets and cover with gravel. Lower to the bottom of the pond and let them grow to the surface. If they grow too much, lift out and trim back.*

The flow down the waterfall

A clear drop here stops water backing up into the filter.

Here the flow is fast and creates the sound of a natural waterfall.

The water falls quite gently into the pond, just rippling the surface.

This pool of slow-moving water is ideal for suitable plants.

1 To add plants to the waterfall, fill the lower pool with washed gravel (ideally with rounded stones in case any sharp pieces fall into the pond) to a depth of about 4cm (1.5in) to allow the plants to root into it. Here, the water flow will be relatively slow.

2 Use easy-to-grow plants such as watercress or mimulus, as either of these plants will grow without soil and will remove nitrates from the water, thus helping to reduce algae growth in the pond. You will need to cut them back regularly, as they grow so fast.

The planted pond

Taller plants such as this Iris pseudacorus *'Variegata', here planted with* Lobelia cardinalis, *add height to the pond planting and, once established, offer useful shade.*

Ranunculus flammula

Hottonia palustris

Lythrum salicaria *'Robert'*

Myosotis palustris

The plants along the front edge of the pond are (left to right): Lobelia *'Fan Deep Red',* Hippuris vulgaris *and* Cotula coronopifolia. *The water lily is* Nymphaea *'Marliacea Albida'.*

*The light green foliage of the umbrella palm (*Cyperus alternifolia*) contrasts with the dark red leaves of* Lobelia cardinalis, *which bears vivid scarlet flowers in midsummer.*

Getting the numbers right

Aim to fill all the space on the marginal shelves. If the pond becomes overcrowded, you can cut back unwanted plants or remove ones that are too vigorous and divide them into smaller plants.

Hints and tips

Do not use pond plants in soilless potting mix, because the lightweight mix will float in the pond and discolour the water. Replant them in a suitable aquatic soil and top them with gravel. As you finish the pond planting, continue the colour scheme into the rockery and garden.

Schoenoplectus *'Albescens', a tall grass with vertical stripes.*

LINER POND - *Adding the fish*

When you are ready to buy your first fish, go on a day when the weather is cool and, if possible, when the aquatic centre is not too busy so you can see the fish and talk to a member of staff. Explain that they are for a new pond and buy just a few hardy goldfish. Do not fill the pond with fish – give it time to settle down. The filter system must mature before it can deal with more than just a few fish.

Only buy fish that look healthy. Do not choose ones lying on their sides or any that stay away from the rest of the fish in a tank. In fact, avoid buying any fish in such a tank on the basis that if one is ill there is a strong possibility that the others are, too. Look for fish with a good colour and that are well fed; do not buy skinny fish. Look at the fish in the bag before you take them home. Are all the fins in good condition? Are there any marks on the fish? If you are doubtful about a particular fish, ask to change it. If you start with healthy fish, you will hopefully keep them and enjoy them for several years.

How many fish will the pond support?

The easiest way to estimate stocking levels is to allow 2cm (0.8in) of fish per 50 litres (11 gallons) of water. This pond holds 2300 litres (505 gallons) of water so the calculation is 2300÷50x2=92cm of fish, or 9 fish each 10cm (4in) long or 5 fish each 20cm (8in) long. However many fish the pond will theoretically hold, always understock to allow the fish to grow to the natural stocking level of the pond. Overcrowding only results in poor growth and outbreaks of disease.

1 Take your fish home as soon as you can. The dealer will put them in a plastic bag with air (or oxygen for long journeys) taking up most of the space in the bag. Keep the bag cool and in a box or covered, as the fish are less stressed in the dark.

2 As soon as you get home, float the bag on the pond with the top still tied. After about 20 minutes, open the bag and let in some pond water – about half as much as in the bag – and tie the top up again. Leave for another 20 minutes.

3 After letting the fish get used to the water, slowly tip the fish and water out into the pond, making sure that all the fish are out of the bag before putting it away. (Keep the bag; you may need it if you have to transport a fish one day.) The fish will hide for a day or two, so there is no need to feed them. After this, feed them once a day to start with, then twice a day.

The completed pond

The final task is to plant the rockery and the surrounding flower bed. There are some plants you should avoid using near liner ponds. These include bamboos, because the roots are very sharp and can puncture the liner. You will need to position a few plants around the filter to hide it – avoid using spiky ones here, as you will have to push them aside to maintain the filter.

Left: When planting along the sides of the waterfall, use low-growing alpines that follow the contours of the rocks, to help hide the edge and any liner that may show. If they are evergreen, they will soften the rockery edges throughout the year.

Plant some evergreen shrubs near the filter to hide it, even in winter.

Try to choose shrubs that provide a spread of flowering times throughout the year.

Take care

Before planting any shrubs near the pond, check that they are not poisonous to fish or pond wildlife, especially if they shed leaves that will fall into the water.

Make sure that soil cannot run into the pond water from the rockery planting. A good way to finish the rockery is with fine gravel – this will stop soil washing down into the pond and suppress weeds at the same time.

Once you have set up your pond and introduced any fish, it is important to monitor the water quality. Like all animals, fish need a healthy environment in which to thrive. Because testing sounds complex, it is often overlooked by beginners, but today it is simplicity itself to check the water quality using a range of test kits available from your aquatic dealer.

Whichever test kit you use, keep a record of your results. As you build up the log, it will be easy to spot trends and you will quickly see if a problem is developing. This means that you can take remedial action straight away and be prepared if the same trend develops again. Always buy the same test kit so that you get accustomed to the colours and test procedures. Here we look at the most vital tests.

Testing for pH

The pH scale measures the acidity or alkalinity of the pond water on a scale running from 0 to 14. Extremely acid conditions would register as 0, neutral as 7 and a very alkaline reading as 14. Pond fish will survive quite happily in water with a pH measuring between 6.5 and 8, but the closer to the neutral value of 7, the better.

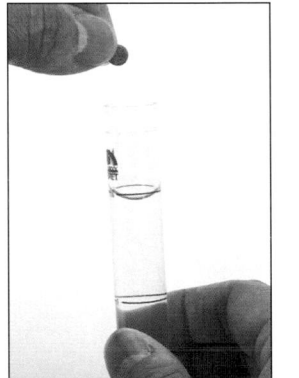

Left: Wash out the glass vial with pond water and fill it to the line as shown. Add the test tablet, put the top on the tube and shake it vigorously. Do not put your finger over the end, as this may affect the result.

Below: Wait for the suggested time for the colour to develop and then compare it with the printed chart. Hold the tube against the white area next to the scale to make an accurate comparison.

Y TEST **2** (NO₂)	EASY TEST **3** NITRATE (NO₃)	EASY TEST **5** pH BROAD RANGE
	mg/litre	pH
	0	4
	10	5
	25	6.5
	50	7
	75	8.5
	100	9
ONS ON USE		

Paper strip test

These test strips are supplied in a container that has the reference colour chart printed on the label. Take out a strip with dry hands and dip it into the water for one second and remove it. Wait for one minute for the colours to develop. Avoid shaking excess water off it, because this may mix up the results. Do not put used strips with new ones.

Right: You can dip the test strip directly into the pond or scoop out a cup or jar of water to make the test.

Right: Compare the strip colours with the chart. From the top these show nitrate, nitrite, total hardness (three squares), carbonate hardness and pH.

Testing for ammonia

Ammonia is produced as fish waste decomposes in the water and is also excreted directly by the fish through their gills. It is one of the compounds in the so-called 'nitrogen cycle' – the constant circulation of nitrogen through plants and animals that occurs in all living environments. The bacteria in a mature biological filter break ammonia down to nitrite. Ammonia is very toxic to fish and any reading is serious. A quick water change is the best way to dilute the ammonia until you can find the cause of the build-up. Usually it is the result of too many fish in a new pond being fed too much. The fish produce large amounts of waste and because the bacteria colonies in the biological filter are not fully developed, they are not able to convert the ammonia into less harmful substances.

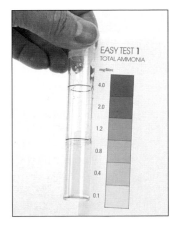

Left: This test involves adding two tablets to a water sample and comparing the colour to a printed chart. This is one of the most important tests to carry out, especially for newly set up ponds. Do the test once a month and if there is a positive reading, test again every day until clear.

Note: There are other tests that you can carry out on pond water, but these are not essential to start with. However, once the 'pond bug' sets in and you become more interested in the subject, you might care to delve further into these.

Testing for nitrite

This is the second stage product of the filter system and can be toxic in high levels over a long period. To reduce levels quickly, make a water change and stop feeding the fish. This stops them producing waste and gives the filter a chance to convert nitrite to nitrate.

Left: Add one tablet to the water sample and shake. The colour takes 10 minutes to develop fully.

Right: Compare the colour in the sample to the printed chart. This reading shows a high level of nitrite.

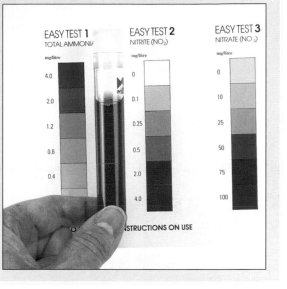

Testing for nitrate

The last product in the nitrogen cycle is relatively non-toxic in low levels and is used as plant food. This is where the plants play a vital role, because they use the nitrate to grow and produce leaves and flowers, thereby preventing nitrate levels from rising.

Left: This water sample is already showing a reaction to the first tablet added. The second tablet being added here completes the colour change for the test.

Right: Comparing this test sample to the chart shows that the pond water has fairly low levels of nitrate, which are not a cause for concern.

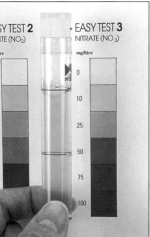

Plants for your pond

One of the most enjoyable stages of pond building is the planting. It gives the pond its final shape and softens the edges of the hard landscaping. The major reasons for adding plants are to provide shade and to help maintain the water quality. Floating and marginal plants both provide shade, which reduces the amount of light reaching the water and hence the growth of algae. Floating plants are important when you first plant the pond because they provide shade until the marginals have developed. As the floaters cover the surface, harvest the excess to prevent total coverage, which would prevent the oxygenators from growing. In later years, as water lilies and other plants mature, you will need fewer floating plants. Growing plants absorb nitrate and carbon dioxide as food and produce oxygen, which helps the fish and reduces algae at the same time.

Trapa natans grows quickly in warm weather. Remove excess plants when they cover the surface. Not frost hardy, so remove it from the pond in winter.

Below: Both azolla and myriophyllum grow quickly and can easily take over a pond if left unchecked. Thin them at regular intervals during the growing season.

Floating plants

Azolla caroliniana
Eichhornia crassipes
Hydrocharis
Pistia stratiotes
Stratiotes aloides

Elodea crispa is one of the most popular oxygenators. On sunny days, you can see bubbles of oxygen rising from it.

Oxygenating plants

Callitriche autumnalis
Ceratophyllum demersum
Elodea canadensis
Elodea crispa
Eleocharis
Fontinalis antipyretica
Hottonia palustris
Myriophyllum spicatum
Potamogeton crispus
Ranunculus aquatilis
Utricularia vulgaris

Suggested marginal plants

Acorus calamus 'Variegatus'
Alisma plantago-aquatica
Butomus umbellatus
Calla palustris
Caltha palustris 'Plena'
Cotula coronopifolia
Cyperus alternifolius
Glyceria maxima var.
  variegata
Houttuynia cordata
Iris laevigata 'Variegata'
Lobelia cardinalis
Lysichiton camtschatcensis
Lythrum salicaria

Lysimachia nummularia
Mentha aquatica
Menyanthes trifoliata
Myosotis 'Mermaid'
Nasturtium officinale
Oenanthe japonica 'Flamingo'
Pontederia cordata
Rumex sanguineus
Sagittaria japonica 'Flore
  Pleno'
Schoenoplectus 'Zebrinus'
Typha minima
Veronica beccabunga
Zantedeschia aethiopica

Butomus umbellatus. *Although not free-flowering when young, it is worth waiting for, as the flowers, offset by dark green foliage, last a long time.*

Above: *The arrowhead-shaped leaves of sagittaria are just part of the attraction of this marginal plant. The summer flowers make it an essential addition to the pond.*

Above: Nymphaea 'James Brydon' is one of the best water lilies you can buy. Even young plants produce cup-shaped, rose-red flowers with medium-round, dark green foliage in summer.

Suggested water lilies

White: *Nymphaea* 'Gonnère' (large), *N. odorata* (medium), *N. odorata* var. *minor* (very small)

Pink: *N.* 'Madame Wilfon Gonnère' (medium/large), *N.* 'Firecrest' (medium), *N.* 'Laydekeri Lilacea' (small)

Red: *N.* 'Escarboucle' (large), *N.* 'James Brydon' (medium), *N.* 'Froebelii' (small)

Yellow: *N.* 'Marliacea Chromatella' (large), *N.* 'Texas Dawn' (large), *N.* 'Odorata Sulphurea' (medium), *N.* 'Pygmaea Helvola' (very small)

Variable colour: 'Sioux' (medium)

Fish for your pond

When the pond has been established with plants for three to four weeks, and providing the test results are all within safe limits, it is time to buy a few fish. They will help the pond to settle down. To start with, add just a few hardy fish to make sure that the water quality is good enough and to help the biofilter to start working. Do not be tempted to stock the pond to its maximum level straightaway, as this will lead to 'new pond syndrome', which happens when the filter is overloaded and cannot cope with the waste produced by the fish; in reality, the fish poison themselves with their own waste. Be patient and add a few fish at a time. See page 46 for a guide to estimating how many fish you can add to the pond.

Regular maintenance

Poor water quality is the chief cause of all problems in ponds, and fish are highly susceptible to it. Get into the habit of checking the pump every day to ensure that it is working smoothly and check the filter once a week. Test the water on a weekly basis in spring and once a month during the rest of the season. The thing to remember is that it is better (and cheaper) in the long run to keep the fish healthy than to spend time trying to treat and sort out problems.

Right: *Goldfish are the most popular and the hardiest pond fish. They are always on the move and their bright colour is very attractive. They make the perfect introduction to pondkeeping.*

Above: *The minnow is ideal for a wildlife pond, as it will eat mosquito larvae, but is too small – it only grows to 10cm (4in) – to eat many of the other pond inhabitants. Being dark in colour, it will not attract herons or other predators.*

Left: *Once the comet tail sarasa has settled down, it makes a stunning addition to the pond. The deep red colour against the snow white skin and the long flowing fins are a pleasure to see as they swim past.*

Below: The green tench helps to keep the bottom of the pond clean. As it turns over the substrate looking for food, it dislodges small particles that collect in the filter. However, you will probably never see this bottom dweller again once it is in the pond.

The fins of a healthy fish are erect and spread out. If they are held against the body, it is a bad sign.

Right: The golden orfe is an excellent shoaling fish, so be sure to keep it in a group of its own kind. It can grow quite large, but is always active, even in winter. As a surface-swimmer, it is always visible and can become the victim of cats if not protected.

Keeping koi

Koi will require more attention than other pond fish, and you will have to spend more time maintaining and cleaning the equipment. When you go on holiday, someone will have to check the pond each day to feed the fish and ensure that nothing goes wrong.

Right: Koi could be described as the king of pond fish, but their large size and fondness for uprooting and eating vegetation make them a difficult fish to keep in planted pools. To see them at their best, keep them in a specialist koi pond.

53

If you can find a shape and size to suit your garden, using a shell offers a convenient and trouble-free way of creating a pond. The good thing about using a shell is that you can move it around the garden and try it in different situations to help you decide on the best position for your pond. The larger sizes can be difficult to handle and so, unless you can get it in the car, arrange for the dealer to deliver the shell, as they will transport it safely, without risk to you or the pond!

This type of fairly rigid plastic shell is ideal for most ponds.

Above: *You can choose from a wide range of preformed plastic modules to create an instant waterfall. Some models have planting pockets built in.*

Glass-reinforced plastic (GRP) shells are available in a wide range of shapes and sizes. They are strong and very durable.

Flexible plastic shells are a cheaper option for small ponds.

Pond shell materials

Pond shells are made in a range of plastics – the most rigid being reinforced with fibreglass. Here we compare the main options. When buying a shell, check for holes and cracks. These allow water to get in and if it freezes the shell will split.

Glass-reinforced plastic (GRP)
An excellent material for pond shells. It is sturdy, weather resistant and can be moulded to any shape and depth.

Firm plastic
Pond shells made of this thick plastic are fine for a wide range of projects. They are strong, long lasting and deep enough for fish to thrive all year.

Flexible plastic
Shells made from this more flexible plastic are usually only available in smaller sizes. They may not be deep enough to overwinter fish.

Positioning the pond shell

Check the preformed shape for any damage or holes. Read any installation instructions that are supplied with the shell and follow any warranty procedures.

When positioning the pond, make sure there are no tree roots or drain runs in the way. You will not be able to bend the pond around an obstacle, as you could with a liner.

Protecting the shell

While you dig the hole, store the pond in a safe place out of the way. Make sure it is not resting on any sharp objects that could puncture it. Ideally, store it indoors or at least out of the wind, as it flies very well! If you have to keep it outdoors, stand it upside down on a soft surface to avoid damage. Place some bags of sand on top to stop the wind lifting and blowing it away. This also prevents it filling with rain, which could pose a hazard if a child fell into the shell.

A RIGID POND SHELL – Digging the hole

1 With the pond in position, lay sand right round the base to mark out the shape. Move the pond shell out of the way so that it is not damaged while you dig the hole.

2 Dig out the marked area plus 5cm (2in) all around to allow for the tapered shape. Excavate the hole to the overall depth of the pond. Remove the spoil from the site.

3 Lower the pond carefully into the excavated hole to the level of the shelves. It is unlikely to fit exactly straight away, so remove the shell and make any adjustments.

4 When you are completely happy with the 'fit', leave the pond in position and mark around the pond with sand as before. This will give you a guide to the final digging stage.

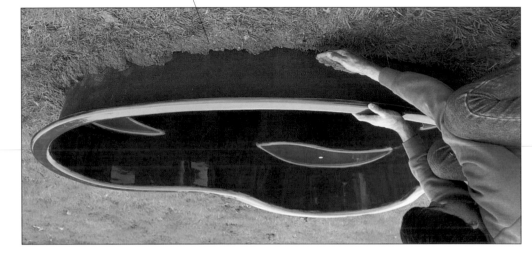

Make this a generous layer of sand; some is bound to fall into the hole when you move the shell.

5 Excavate the entire area to the maximum depth of the pond, plus 5cm (2in) to allow for a sand layer, plus the thickness of the stone paving. Dig up to the sand mark, plus about 5cm (2in) to allow for the tapered pond shape and to give you room to backfill with sand.

Dig out any shelves, following the shape and depth of the shell, plus an extra 5cm (2in) to allow for the sand base and backfill.

If you are not using the spoil as the foundation of a waterfall or rockery feature, remove it as you work.

Safety first

Digging a hole this size is hard work. Do not rush to finish, take frequent breaks and drink plenty of fluids if the weather is warm. Use a spade that is strong enough to cope with the work. If the digging is too much for you, hire a small mechanical digger and dumper. These will fit through narrow side gates; check with your local hire shop.

A RIGID POND SHELL – Completing the excavation

As you come to the end of the excavation process, check the hole for tree roots and stones and remove any that are visible. Tree roots can be a problem around pond shells. Although they rarely puncture the shell, cut roots tend to regrow, producing many smaller ones that can push in the sides of the pond and, in the case of smaller ponds, even lift them up. This can put a great strain on the pond and lead to cracks and leaking. To avoid this risk, cut any roots back as far as possible into the soil and place some thick plastic on the end of the root. This will stop it growing towards the pond. Firm down the soil before adding any sand.

1 With the hole fully excavated, trim back the edge at an angle, so that you can backfill the hole with sand. This is necessary because preformed ponds have a lip around the edge.

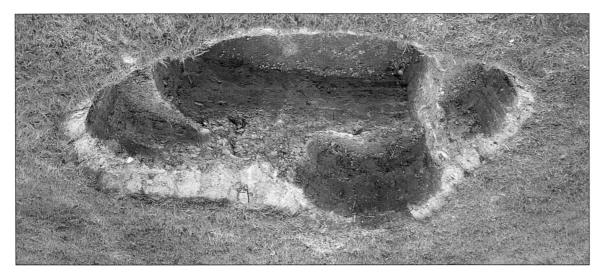

2 Cover the shelves with a good layer of building sand 5-6.5cm (2-2.5in) thick. Make sure there are no stones or other sharp objects in it that might damage the shell.

3 Also cover the base with sand and rake it level, again checking for stones. It is important that the shell sits on a firm base of sand to cushion it safely when it is full of water.

4 Lift the pond into the sanded hole. Take great care not to knock any soil or other debris into the hole as you go. This task is much easier to do with two people.

5 Once you have placed the pond in the hole, press it down around the edge, remove it and check to make sure the pond is sitting on all the sanded areas. If not, add more sand. Look around the edge of the pond for marks to see if the pond is resting or rubbing on the soil. Trim back any areas of soil to allow the sand to fill the gap when backfilling.

Supporting the shell with sand

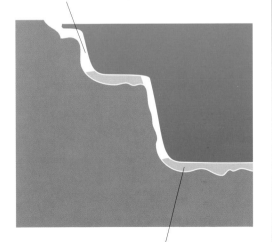

You can fill up this area with sand once the shell is in position.

Make sure the shell sits firmly on a thick bed of sand across the base of the hole.

A RIGID POND SHELL – Levelling and backfilling

Making sure that the pond shell is level is the most important stage of the installation process. Spend as much time as you can getting it right, as it will affect the final appearance of the pond. When the pond is finished and landscaped, there is nothing more unattractive than seeing 10cm (4in) of shell protruding at one end and only 1cm (0.4in) at the other because the pond shell is not level. Be patient, check, check and check again until you get it right. Although this seems time-consuming and laborious, it will save you time and effort in the end, because if you fail to get it right at this stage, you may have to empty the pond and do it all again. If you are unsure about any aspect of the installation, check with your supplier before you go any further. If they cannot help, speak to the manufacturers.

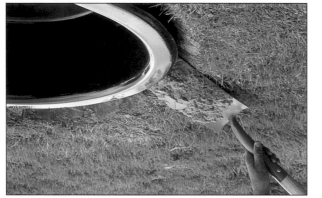

2 Check the level again, this time across the width of the shell. Adjust it if necessary by lifting the pond out carefully and adding more sand. You can see where the pond has been resting because it leaves marks on the sand.

1 With the pond in place, check that it is level along the length. This is absolutely vital: if the pond is not level, it will be very obvious when it is full of water and this could ruin the whole appearance of the finished pond.

3 Backfill with sand or sifted earth, making sure there are no stones or lumps in it, as these will show through the sides as small bulges. As you backfill, add water to the pond to stop the sand lifting the pond out of the ground.

4 When the backfilling is complete, dig a trench around the pond to install a base for the paving. Make it a little narrower than the paving you intend to use. If you are using stone, you can cut the pieces to fit the base. Follow the directions for making a concrete collar given on pages 17-19. Leave a cavity to accommodate a filter, as described on page 63.

5 Once the concrete is dry, lay the paving on a bed of mortar. This stone paving is a natural product that varies in thickness, so increase the depth of the mortar under the thinner pieces. Use different sizes and shapes of stone for a 'crazy paving' effect. Slope the paving away from the pond to stop water draining into it when it rains.

How much paving will I need?

When you have dug the base for the paving, measure around the pond, following a line midway across the collar. Then measure the maximum width of the collar. Multiply the two measurements together to give you the area of paving needed.

For example, if the distance around the pond is 7m and the maximum width of the collar is 0.65m, multiply 7x0.65. This gives an area of 4.55 square metres (about 50 sq ft) and that is how much paving you will need.

6 There are two ways of pointing between the paving. The more traditional method is to point with a trowel, as shown here, which will produce a raised finish. Alternatively, you can use a piece of hose to produce a flush surface as shown on page 31.

The advent of new moulding techniques has allowed manufacturers to produce improved filters that are simple to use and maintain. This model can be fitted below water level, so it is easy to hide from view. It combines all the most desirable features: water pumped from the pond into the filter is forced through a foam block, which extracts floating particles. The bacteria colonising the foam convert toxic waste products into plant food. The cleaned water then passes a UV bulb that kills off algae and parasites, keeping the pond clear and healthy.

Combined biofilter and UV steriliser

The foam in this filter provides not only mechanical, but also biological filtration.

This unit houses the ultraviolet (UV) bulb and the electrical connections to run it.

The UV unit and foam fit into this canister. The hand-operated clips around the edge make it easy to open and clean.

Cleaned water returns to the pond through here.

Below: *Always read the instructions supplied before installing any new product. The connections may not always be what you expect.*

Dirty water is pumped from the pond and enters the unit here.

The three hosetails supplied give you a choice of hose sizes. For best flow rates, use the largest that your pump will take.

This is the UV bulb. Do not turn it on without water running through the system and never look at without eye protection.

Housing the filter unit in the collar

This pipe carries cleaned water away from the filter and back into the pond via the ornamental fish spout.

Use a slab to cover the cavity housing the filter.

This pipe carries water from the pond pump to the filter.

2 Select a piece of stone to cover the filter. Lay a bed of mortar around the filter without affecting access to it, lay the stone in place and level as normal. Leave it for a few minutes, lift it out and allow the mortar to set overnight. This will create a cover that you can lift out and replace as necessary.

Pond shell

Sand layer

Concrete collar

Because the combined filter/UV unit is pressurised, you can hide it below water level.

1 When concreting the collar, you can leave a hole for the combined biofilter and UV unit to fit into (see diagram). With the pipework connected, lower the filter into the cavity without bending or crushing the pipes.

Before selecting a pump, decide what demands you are going to make on it. Is it going to supply a simple fountain or a complex filter system? Do not choose on price alone; look at the quality and enquire about the availability of spares. Make sure the pump and filter are compatible. Ask the retailer for advice if necessary. If water is to flow through an ornament, choose the feature before buying the pump. Filter manufacturers will recommend a flow rate; do not exceed this, thinking that the filter will work better.

Parts of a pump

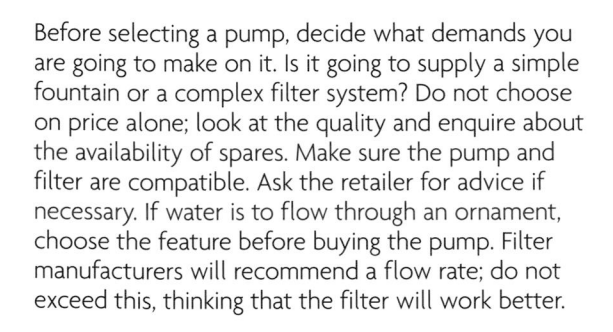

The casing encloses the motor, impeller and the pre-filter.

Flexible hose

Always use the correct size stainless steel clips.

Use this adjuster to regulate water flow to the fountain and filter.

1 Assemble the fountain head and T-piece. Connect the hose to the side hosetail. Use the largest diameter flexible hose that will fit the pump.

2 Tighten up the hose clip enough to stop the hose from being pulled off. Do not overtighten it, as you will risk breaking the hosetail.

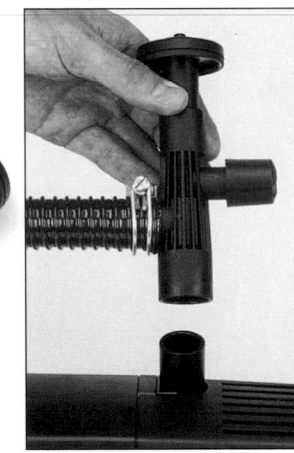

3 Push the T-piece onto the pump outlet. You can fit an extension tube to raise the fountain head to the desired height. (We have fitted a very long extension tube on the pump being installed in the GRP shell shown below.)

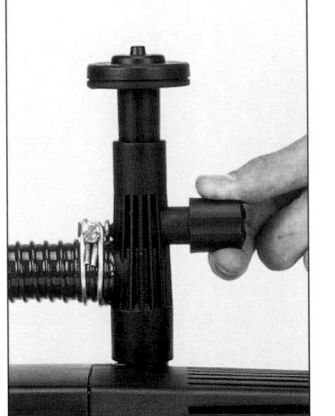

4 The fountain regulator valve also controls the water to the filter. As the flow to the fountain is reduced, more water goes to the filter and vice versa.

5 Install the pump before connecting it to the electrical supply. You may need an extension tube if the fountainhead does not reach above the surface. Connect the hose to the pump with a stainless steel hose clip. Make sure you connect to the inlet of the filter and not the outlet.

6 You can hide the return pipe from the filter to the pond by connecting it to an ornament, such as this fish. As well as hiding the return, it can also hide the pipes as they go under the edge of the stone paving.

How the water flows

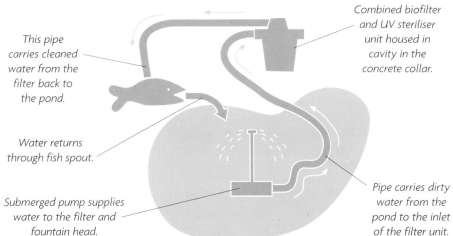

This pipe carries cleaned water from the filter back to the pond.

Combined biofilter and UV steriliser unit housed in cavity in the concrete collar.

Water returns through fish spout.

Submerged pump supplies water to the filter and fountain head.

Pipe carries dirty water from the pond to the inlet of the filter unit.

Once the filter and pumps are working, you can add some oxygenators and marginals. A fountain will disturb the water surface and most water lilies will not do well in these conditions. As an alternative, plant either *Nuphar japonica* or *Aponogeton distachyos*, both of which tolerate this water movement. If you really want a water lily, select a fountain that does not splash much, such as a water bell or foaming jet.

Right: With water running through the ornament, check that the flow rate through the filter is high enough. Time how long it takes to fill a 10-litre (2-gallon) bucket. From this you can work out the flow rate.

Above: *Fish are very popular stone ornaments and vary in style from this Chinese-type design to the more modern one we have used in the shell pond.*

Left: Take into account the height of an ornament. This will affect how much the water splashes as it returns to the pond.

Right: Frogs are popular pondside ornaments. Here, the inlet pipe is visible in the base.

Take note

Make sure that the pipe running through these features is big enough to maintain the flow rate from the filter. If not, connect the feature separately to the pond pump.

A sparkling display

When the paving is finished, tidy up the edges by filling any spaces with soil so that the grass grows up to the edge.

Make sure the ornament does not spray water out of the pond if you alter the fountain flow rate.

Juncus effusus 'Spiralis'

Hippuris vulgaris

A good mixture of water plants will ensure a varied display of foliage and flowers throughout the season.

Houttuynia cordata *Variegata Group*

Myosotis

Schoenoplectus (Scirpus) 'Albescens'

Many pumps are now supplied with two or three fountain heads so that you can change them to vary the spray pattern.

Rumex sanguineus

Myosotis scorpioides 'Mermaid'

Cyperus alternifolia

When choosing a pond for the patio, consider exactly what you intend to keep in it. If it is to house fish over the winter, you may need to put insulation material between the shell pond and the walling to stop the pond freezing in cold weather. If you want to keep plants, use some bricks or extra pots to raise the plants to the correct depth in the water. Try not to place the pond where it will be in full sun all day, as it will overheat. On the other hand, in complete shade, the plants will not flower as well as they should. A deeper pond will give better results and is more difficult for small children to climb into. Most importantly, the patio must be level and able to support the weight of the pond, the walling and the water. Lastly, make sure that there is an electrical supply within easy reach.

2 Stand the pond in the required position and start to lay out the walling. New, shaped materials make working with circles and irregular shapes much easier. Many of the new products available can be dry laid (without mortar), but if you have children you can buy a stone glue to secure the walling for added safety.

1 If you create a patio pond using any form of rigid shape, make sure that the shell is self-supporting so that the wall need not take any weight. This makes the installation much easier.

3 As you lay each course, be sure to overlap each section of walling by half to give a neat appearance and increase the strength of the wall. If you are fixing the walling sections together, wipe off any excess glue as you go. This will stop any stains appearing or glue running down the walling.

Make sure that the edge of the coping overlaps both the outer edge of the walling and the outside edge of the pond shell.

The finishing touch to the wall is the coping, which should overlap the joints below by half.

Once you have decided what you are going to keep in your pond, you can buy the appropriate pump. If you intend to keep fish, choose a combined pump and filter to enhance the water quality and reduce maintenance. There are many models on sale. The most basic types incorporate a large piece of plastic foam that fits onto the front of the pump. More sophisticated models feature combined biofilters and ultraviolet light units. If you just want to grow plants, a simple fountain pump will be fine and you can change the fountain heads to suit the mood and weather – taller fountains will lose more water in windy conditions.

Pumps and fountains

Three-tier fountain head

Mains fountain pump and strainer

Adjustable fountain extension and flow valve

Bell fountain head

1 When installing a fountain pump, be sure to disconnect it from the electricity before you start. If necessary, lengthen the cable with the proper connectors to reach the power supply. If you are not sure what to do, use a low-voltage pump, which is easy to install and safe to operate.

Above: *Depending on the pump/fountain design, you may need to raise the pump off the bottom in order for the fountain to work correctly. As small pumps weigh very little, sit them on a solid base of bricks or on an upturned terracotta pot.*

This pump is sitting on the base at the correct height for the fountain head.

3 Once installed, switch on the pump and adjust the fountain so that the spray falls within the pond. When planting the pond, use taller-growing plants placed on bricks or upturned pots. If you have a fountain, remember that water lilies do not like water falling on their leaves.

Right: Fountain patterns, such as this water bell, are ideal for patio or ponds in windy situations. Adjust the diameter and height of the bell to suit the pond.

2 Start to fill the pond with water, but do not switch on the pump until it is completely submerged, otherwise you will damage the internal mechanism.

Spring

Spring is the busiest time of year for the pondkeeper. Start by removing any nets that you put over the pond the previous autumn to catch falling leaves. As far as plants are concerned, this is the time to replace bog and marginal plants that have died or outgrown their welcome. If necessary, remove the plants, divide them and then repot them ready for the season ahead.

Check fish for signs of disease and treat them once the water temperature has risen above 10°C (50°F). You can start feeding the fish at the same time.

Now is also the time to reinstate the filter system. Replace the UV bulb, clean the pump, test it and set it running. Leave it running continuously. Refer to the manufacturer's instructions for more guidance. Clean the paving around the pond and remove any leaves, so that there is no danger of people slipping over. If necessary, clean out the pond completely and refill it. You should not have to do this every year unless the pond is very full of decaying leaves.

Identifying sick fish

Sick fish tend to hang in one area of the pond, away from the rest of the fish. They will not eat, and if they are very sick, may even allow them-selves to be picked up. Look out for any sign of damaged fins and growths on the body of the fish.

Above: *One of the first aquatic plants to signal spring is* Caltha palustris, *the marsh marigold. Deadhead it once the flowers are over to encourage it to flower again.*

Right: *In the boggy margins of the pond, primulas provide bright splashes of colour against the darker leaves of other plants emerging during the spring.*

Summer

In summer, pond plants grow rapidly and will need plenty of attention. Remove any weeds, deadhead self-seeding plants before they shed their seed and cut back invasive plants before they become a problem. Add new plants, including water lilies. It is a good idea to feed new plants to help them become established and to encourage good growth. Trim oxygenating plants as they grow, to encourage new,

Below: During the summer, the combination of heat and thundery weather can cause low oxygen levels in the pond. Keep the fountain going to get more oxygen into the water.

more vigorous growth. Watch out for pests on the plants; you cannot spray them if there are fish in the pond, so remove any infected leaves or wash off the pests with a strong water jet.

Remove algae as it develops. Adding barley straw to the pond helps to suppress the growth of blanketweed.

Check the condition of the pump prefilter (the foam block in the pump) and clean it as necessary. Most pumps incorporate an overflow system and this will give you a good indication when the filter needs cleaning. If water starts to run down the overflow, it means that the foams are too dirty for the water to pass through them. Clean them straightaway to restore the water flow.

You will also need to clean the foam layers in the biofilter on a regular basis. Fill a bucket with pond water and wash the foams in this to avoid killing off the beneficial bacteria that are living within them.

At this time of year, it is a good idea to offer the fish smaller amounts of feed two or three times a day, rather than one large feed. Fish spend most of their time feeding and have a very short digestive cycle. This means that if you offer them large amounts of food at once, much of it will pass through the fish undigested and is therefore wasted.

Add new fish, but monitor them carefully for signs of disease. Keep the pump running during thundery weather to keep the water well oxygenated; low oxygen levels will kill the fish.

Right: During the first few months as the pond plants become established, you may need to remove algae from the water as it builds up. Twirl it round a stick, but be careful not to wind up any fish or frogs.

Right: Feed aquatic plants in baskets with slow-release fertiliser pellets. Do this after they have flowered, because some plants will not flower if there is an excess of feed.

Autumn

When autumn arrives, water lily leaves turn yellow-brown. Cut the foliage of all submerged plants back hard so that it does not die in winter and pollute the pond. Cut away the leaves and stalks of marginal plants and remove all rotting material from the pond. Remove any tender plants that you may have added in summer and overwinter them in frost-free conditions for the following season.

Feed the fish well to prepare them for the winter hibernation ahead. Once the fish have stopped feeding in late autumn or early winter (depending on the temperature), drain the filters, remove any UV systems and store them indoors. Clean the pump and remove it if necessary.

Cover the pond with netting to catch falling leaves and other debris and to stop animals falling in.

Left: Scoop up any leaves from the pond soon after they fall in. Leaving them to decay may pollute the water and upset the fish.

Below: During the autumn, cut back dead flower stems and leaves to prevent a build-up in the pond.

Winter

In winter, the fish stop feeding as the temperature drops to about 5°C (40°F), and they will not require feeding again until the weather warms up in spring. Cover any tender plants, such as gunnera, with old leaves or straw to protect them from frost. In very severe weather, you will need to create a hole in the ice that forms on the pond to allow toxic gases to escape. This will also prevent the ice expanding and damaging the pond edging. During prolonged cold periods, install a floating electric heater. Never break the ice by striking it; the shock waves could kill the fish. Pour on hot water to create an opening.

Polystyrene float

Using a pond heater

Pond heaters are low wattage and should not be left running continuously unless the weather is extremely cold. Turn them on at night, when the temperature falls to its lowest value. Never run them from an extension power lead; follow the supplier's instructions. The polystyrene float stops the heating element touching — and possibly melting — the liner. Tether the heater to help stop this happening.

The heating element hangs vertically in the water.

Above: *A frozen pond can look elegant, but it is vital for fishes' health to keep an opening in the ice to allow gases to pass into and out of the water. Do not use a floating ball or plastic container because they will not allow gaseous exchange; use a porous polystyrene ice vent or floating pond heater instead.*

INDEX

Page numbers in **bold** indicate major entries; *italics* refer to captions and annotations; plain type indicates other text entries.

CREDITS

The majority of the photographs featured in this book have been taken by Geoffrey Rogers and are © Interpet Publishing.

The publishers would like to thank the following photographers for providing images, credited here by page number and position: B(Bottom), T(Top), C(Centre), BL(Bottom Left), etc.

Eric Crichton: Copyright page, 6, 8(L,C), 9(R), 10, 73(L), 74(BR)

John Glover: 9(BL), 11(L,R), 72(C,R)

S & O Mathews: 74(L), 75(R)

Clive Nichols: 9(TL, Mill House, Sussex), 12(Mill House, Sussex)

PHOTOMAX: 52(BL), 53(TL,TR,B)

Neil Sutherland © Geoffrey Rogers: Title page, contents page (TR), 13(BR), 51(BL, TR)

W A Tomey: 52(BR)

The artwork illustrations have been prepared by Stuart Watkinson and are © Interpet Publishing.

Thanks are due to Blagdon Garden Products Ltd., Bridgewater, Somerset; The Dorset Water Lily Company, Halstock, Dorset; Hozelock Cyprio, Haddenham, Buckinghamshire; Tetra UK, Eastleigh, Hampshire; Chris Newnham and Washington Garden Centre, West Sussex for their help during the preparation of this book.